Origami
Flowers

Fold Beautiful Paper Bouquets

Origami Flowers

Fold Beautiful Paper Bouquets

Table of Contents

65 Practical Flowers

<Extras>

Bonus Origami Paper

○ How to Use Bonus Paper

Cut paper from book and use to create origami flowers. Follow instructions on p 79 for how to cut paper neatly, and cut to the necessary size.

● About the Instructions

The origami designs are marked as indicated by one of three levels of difficulty. The level is shown under the title of the design in the instructions.
(1) Easy
(2) Normal
(3) Difficult

● About Paper Sizing

The instructions for each design list the paper size used to create the final origami shown in the photos. In the case of several sizes, the most convenient size is listed. For instructions that have photos, the paper is the standard 15 x 15 cm size.

The Joy of Origami Flowers: Stimulate Your Brain While Having Fun

Kyorin University
Professor of Neuropsychiatry
Yoshihiko Koga

 ## An Active Brain Prevents Aging

When our brains are at rest, they age. When it comes to the brain, lack of use doesn't mean replenishment. Even when your brain is overworked and you're stressed out, simple rest doesn't dispel fatigue. It's far better to do something else—read a book, do housework, write. As we grow older and the brain begins to slow down, transitioning from a "sleeping" brain to an "active" one is the best way to resist the aging process.

 ## Origami is Moderate, Everyday Exercise that Works the Whole Brain

Origami uses all parts of the brain in a balanced way. Working with your hands exercises the frontal lobe, seeing the design works the occipital lobe, perceiving a three-dimensional object uses the parietal lobe, and remembering colors and shapes requires the temporal lobes.

Also, in order to get your brain into active mode, instead of working it for long stretches, it's better to do something stimulating every day. That's what makes origami perfect. It's not too difficult, it doesn't take much time, and you end up with something to show for it. The focus of your interest changes if you work on a different design each day, so you don't get bored. It doesn't tire you out. Origami is an ideal method of keeping your brain active without a hassle.

 ## Enjoying Origami Reduces Stress

I mentioned that using your head to do something else reduces stress, and folding origami helps to clear your mind even when you're agitated. Letting that stress dissipate is just a wonderful feeling. It puts you in a good mood. Having something to look forward to each day has an excellent anti-aging effect on the brain.

Brain Parts Used When Folding Origami

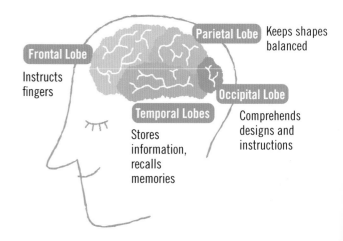

The Three Simple Joys of Origami Flowers

 ## Flowers Bring Back Pleasant Memories

Flowers bring joy from simply looking at them but also from growing them. Yet, gardening is hard work. With origami, however, you can relish bringing flowers into existence too. In addition, being reminded of their vivid colors and pretty shapes will connect with happy memories. Can't you just picture the situation at that certain moment, what your family was doing, each person's face? That's the other appeal of Origami Flowers.

1. The Joy of Creating

Giving shape to a sheet of paper is quite mysterious and exciting. With ceramics, for example, you'd need equipment, and the effort and technique required are nothing to sneeze at. But with origami, you don't need any special prep, and anyone can start immediately and be done in no time. Even so, it's just as thrilling when you finish. With Origami Flowers, you can also relive your happy memories of a season while you're at it.

2. The Joy of Giving

Origami Flowers make inexpensive handmade gifts. They impose no burden on the recipient, who's allowed to simply appreciate it. Getting gifts that don't suit your tastes can be uncomfortable, but everyone takes to flowers, and since it's origami these won't wilt. They're appropriate for people in the hospital too. Some origami flowers can look childish, but the lovely designs in this book are intended to satisfy adult sensibilities.

3. The Joy of Using

Using something that you like vivifies your everyday life. When you eat, how your table is set can make a difference. Owning a collection of fine china is a costly challenge and it's a pain to clean afterwards. But origami dishes shaped like flowers are easy to make and discard time and again. Daily activities can quickly get monotonous, so cherish opportunities to use even a small something that brings you joy.

Lighthearted Communication Using Origami

 ## As an Ice-Breaker

Origami can be a very natural way to engage in positive communication. Aside from making them with others, finished works can be a great conversation piece. Showing how to make origami to family, friends, and even little kids keeps the dialogue going.

 ## For Making Friends

With origami, even if you follow a pattern you can add a personal twist. Your choices as to the kind of paper, color scheme, and final touch amount to a subtle self-presentation. When you make new friends, try giving them something you made. You can put your heart into it without bracing over it and reach out without coming on too hard, helping you build friendships.

 ## For Hosting

Origami Flowers are also helpful when you invite people over for tea or dinner. Place your works tastefully or even as part of the table setting for a hospitable atmosphere. Both you and your guests are bound to start chatting. What's also great is that you can let your guests take your origami home if they like it.

As you can see, the origami in this book serve all kinds of useful and enjoyable functions. Please pick a design you like and get started right away. I hope this book keeps your brain lively and active and your daily life bright and cheerful.

"The joy of origami keeps you hale even as you get older. Interact across generations and borders."

Origami can be crafted at any age, but it's not until you're an adult that you can truly appreciate its pleasures and depth. Don't just rely on old favorites; try designs that are new and a first to watch the world of origami unfold before you. At the Ochanomizu Origami Hall, where we've removed all restrictions, our motto is "Papercraft you can enjoy even if you live to a hundred." We get lots of guests, from the elderly to kids.

Origami is a traditional Japanese craft that can be transmitted overseas. I myself have hosted origami exhibits around the world. A noticeably large contingency of tourists from abroad visit our Origami Hall and genuinely seem to enjoy the displays and crafting their own works.

Ochanomizu Origami Hall
Chairman

Kazuo Kobayashi

Add Color to Your Lifestyle

Seasonal Flowers

The beauty of the four seasons is on display as
flowers bloom in turn in response to shifting sunlight.
Try crafting an origami version of a flower you saw on your
walk, or enjoy the coming season before anyone else.

Spring

Springtime feels fresh and brings cheer no matter what age you are. In Japan, it's the time of flower-viewing parties and the start of a new school year. Fold these origami as those springtime memories bring you joy.

Cherry Blossom

The cherry blossom's familiar silhouette brings instant delight in Japan. Just fold and cut for a surprisingly pretty shape that's easy to make.

● Instructions p 20

Dandelion

Dandelions are at their peak during springtime strolls or trips, so you tend to see them often. Be sure to include the leaves to make it look like these are growing out of the ground.

● Instructions p 21

Standing Tulip

This design bursts with sweet
vitality as if standing tall out of
the earth. The leaves and stem that
support the bloom are key, but it's
easier to make than it seems!

● **Instructions p 22**

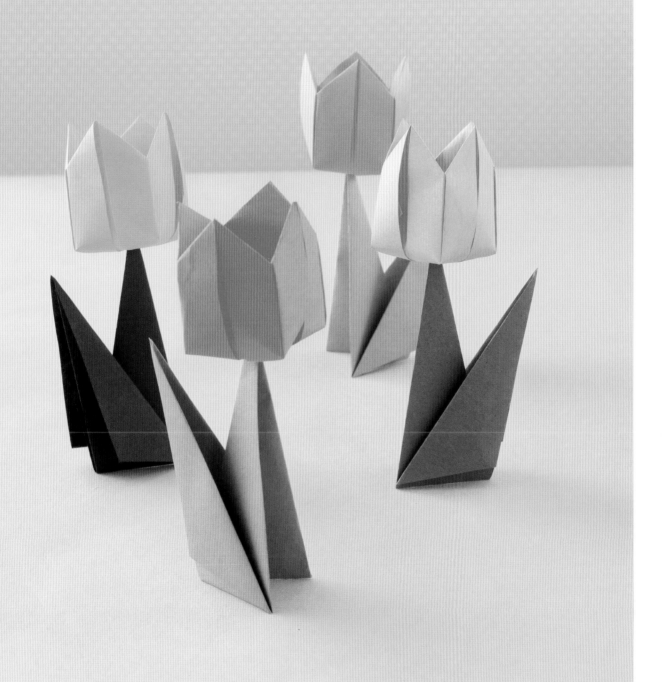

Morning Glory

These cheerful morning glories have white centers that remind you of the sun during summer vacation. Since they're very easy to make, try using a variety of colors and sizes.

● Instructions p 23

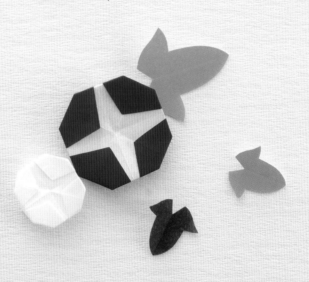

Iris

Purple is the obvious choice for irises, but dark and light blues and reds look great, too. The pointed sepals are gallant, making these a great choice for boys as well as for adults.

● Instructions p 24

Summer

The mighty flowers of summer give an even more cheerful impression when crafted from brightly-colored paper. On the other hand, paper with gradations lend a classy air to the finished piece.

Sunflower

Craft this origami while imagining a real, large sunflower reflecting the sun's rays back up to the sky.
Use paper with a pattern that mimics seeds for the center. The powerful, large leaves are also a key point.

● Instructions p 25

Autumn

The clear, bright skies of autumn make the season's flowers all the more attractive.
These designs for chrysanthemums and cosmos take a new approach to depicting the thin petals.
Experience the depth of the art of origami.

Chrysanthemum

The flower petals and leaves are made entirely of paper cranes to create a large-scale flower. Make wide-winged cranes with diamond-shaped papers and curl up to approximate the weight and presence of the real thing. Make twenty to wish someone a happy recovery.

● Instructions p 26

Cosmos

Lovely cosmos, undulating in the
breeze. Use papers that have a subtle
pattern for an interesting variant.
The thin leaves which are crafted
together with the stem are twisted
to give a sense of movement.

● Instructions p 28

Camellia

Use glossy, sturdy paper to recreate the elegance of camellias with their plump, thick petals and profound color contrasts. The dark, uniquely-shaped leaves are depicted as well.

● **Instructions p 29**

Winter

The flowers of winter stand strong against the chill, captivating all who see them.
The camellia, beloved in Japan since antiquity, and the Christmas-themed poinsettia both feature a symbolically rich red.

Poinsettia

Poinsettias, with some leaves
that stay green and others that
turn red, is the very picture of
Christmastime. These look tough
to make but the instructions are
surprisingly simple, and assembling
the pieces to create the finished
flower will make you happy.

● **Instructions p 30**

New Year

Even without a magnificent evergreen, you can still ring in the new year. Just add an origami daffodil to a sprig of pine. The color will stay fresh and vivid even if you leave it up for several weeks.

Flight of the Cranes

Cranes have featured heavily in Shinto rituals and major familial ceremonies since olden times. This design with two cranes on an envelope enclosing a pine branch features a traditional style of origami.

● For reference

Daffodil

The signatures of daffodils, which begin to bloom around lakes in early spring, are their six petals. Since the flowers portend the coming of spring, they're apt New Year's decorations. Add wire to the leaves to create lean curves.

● Instructions p 32

Legend

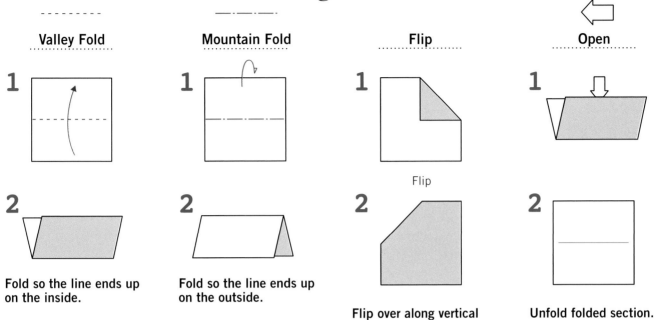

Valley Fold

1

2

Fold so the line ends up on the inside.

Mountain Fold

1

2

Fold so the line ends up on the outside.

Flip

1

Flip

2

Flip over along vertical (but not horizontal) axis.

Open

1

2

Unfold folded section.

Basic Instructions

Here's an explanation of common symbols and folds used in the origami in this book.
The colored side is the front, and the white is the reverse.

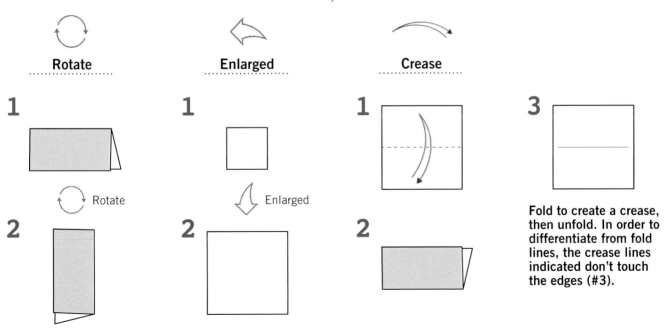

Rotate

1

Rotate

2

Enlarged

1

Enlarged

2

Crease

1

2

3

Fold to create a crease, then unfold. In order to differentiate from fold lines, the crease lines indicated don't touch the edges (#3).

★ When instructions indicate "Fold to the center," lightly crease in half widthwise and lengthwise to mark the center, then fold in.
★ Where instructions indicate a fold to a certain point (marked with a circle), measure with a ruler and either crease lightly or use a pencil to lightly mark the spot before folding so it doesn't show in the final work.
★ Instructions list the sizes upon finishing, but there may be variations due to paper thickness so sizes are approximate.

Legend

Pleat Fold

1

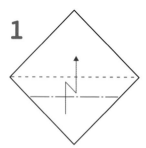

2

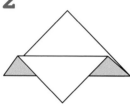

A mountain fold combined with a valley fold to create a pleat.

Roll Fold

1

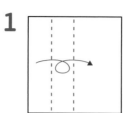

2

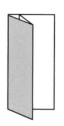

Repeat valley folds as if rolling the paper.

Equal Fold

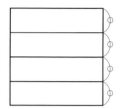

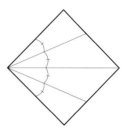

Create folds at even spaces or angles.

Cut

1

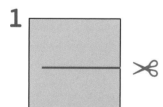

2

Make incisions or remove sections of paper.

Insert

1

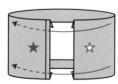

2

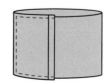

Insert ☆ section into ★ section.

Basic Folds

Square Fold

1

With the front facing you, valley fold along diagonals to crease.

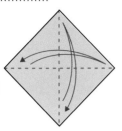

Flip

2

Flip. Valley fold along dashed lines twice as shown to crease.

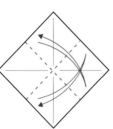

3

Fold in along creases so the three ★ align with ☆.

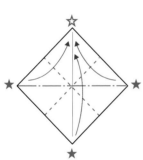

Folding

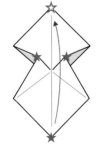

Done

Triangle Fold

1

With the front facing you, valley fold along dashed lines twice as shown to crease.

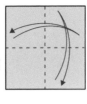

Flip

2

Flip. Valley fold along diagonals to crease.

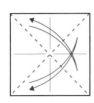

3

Fold in along creases so the three ★ align with ☆.

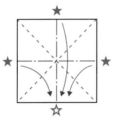

Folding

Done

Outside Reverse Fold

1

Valley fold to crease.

2

Open corner slightly and fold back along creases so the reverse faces out.

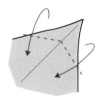

Done

Inside Reverse Fold

1

Fold to crease.

2

Open corner slightly and fold so corner is inside.

Done

Cherry Blossom ● Photos p 8, 46, 69, 70

Difficulty >> 😊 😊 😊

Paper size: 8 x 8 cm
Finished size: 7 x 7 cm

Advice

Fold and cut to create these cherry blossoms. You can keep the sides equal without using a ruler by creasing the center first.

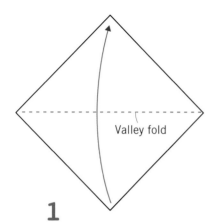

1

Flip over paper and fold in half.

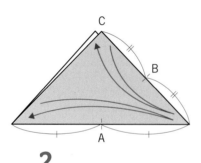

2

On two edges, crease at midpoints A and B.

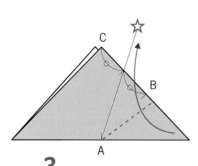

3

Mark the midpoint between B and C. Pick up bottom right corner and valley fold along dashed line to match line from A to ☆.

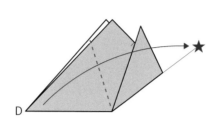

4

Valley fold bottom left corner D to ★ along dashed line.

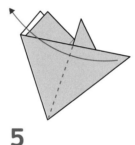

5

Lifting just the top layer, valley fold along dashed line.

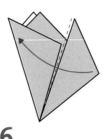

6

Once again, valley fold firmly along dashed line.

Flip

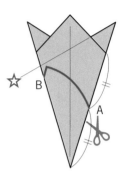

7

Flip over and cut along solid line with line ☆ as a guide. Cut from A, then from B. You can trace the line with a pencil.

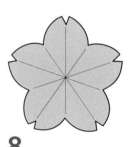

8

Unfold and you're done.

Dandelion ● Photo p 9

Difficulty >> 😊 😊 😊

Paper size: Flower: 7 x 7 cm
Sepal: 6 x 6 cm
Leaves: 6 x 14 cm, 1 to 2 sheets
Finished size: Flower, 4 cm diam.; 20 cm total

Photo p 9

Flower

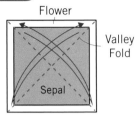

Flower
Valley Fold
Sepal

1

On the reverse of the Flower paper, glue the Sepal paper facing front. Fold to crease both papers.

Flip

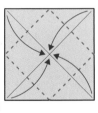

2

Flip over. Fold all four corners to the center.

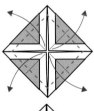

3

Pick up corners in the center and valley fold, with the crease just inside of the edges.

Flip

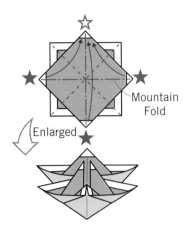

☆
★ Mountain Fold ★
Enlarged
★

4

Flip over. Mountain and valley fold where indicated, folding up so the ★ align with ☆.

5

Open up and fold all four corners in as if squashing.

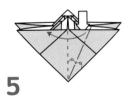

6

Open from top and revert shape to step 3.

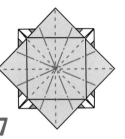

7

Fold up along dashed lines.

8

Firmly fold entire piece in half.

9

Inside reverse fold bottom corner (see p 19).

10

Pinch folded corner. Unfold top sections into flower shape.

Done

Leaves

1

Stack papers, facing front, and fold in half.

2

Cut along solid line. You can trace the pattern with a pencil.

3

Unfold and separate. Fold each piece in half along width at an angle.

Done

Standing Tulip ● Photo p 9

Difficulty >> 😊 😊 😊

Paper: Flower: 15 x 15 cm
Leaves : 15 x 15 cm
Finished size: 15 cm tall

Advice

Use creases to fold. Double-check each mountain and valley fold.

Flower

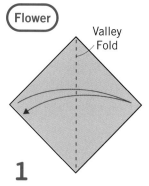

Valley Fold

1

With front up, crease in half along the length.

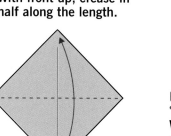

2

Fold along width.

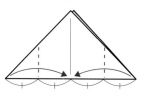

3

Fold in side corners to center.

4

Fold up bottom corners. Unfold entirely and repeat steps 2 through 4 so the area marked ○ looks the same. Unfold entirely.

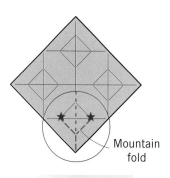

Mountain fold

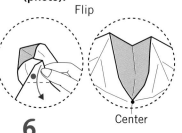

Flip   Center

5

With front up, confirming mountain and valley creases, lift up from reverse side so that the ★ align (photo).

6

Pinch section marked with ● on reverse side and fold in half along crease so the tip aligns with center. Repeat from step 5 with three remaining sides.

Done

Leaves

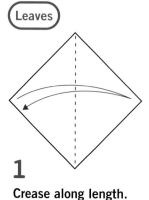

1

Crease along length.

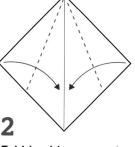

2

Fold in side corners to align with center.

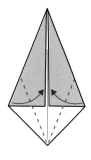

3

Fold in new corners to center as well.

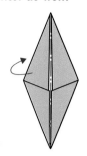

4

Mountain fold so left half is on bottom.

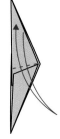

5

Crease all of it along line.

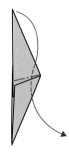

6

Fold down top corner in between stacked sides.

7

Open slightly. Turn up.

↻ Rotate

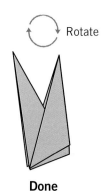

Done

Morning Glory ● Photo p 10

Difficulty >> 😊 😊 😊

Paper size: Flower, 7 x 7 cm; Leaves, 5 x 5 cm
Finished size: Flower, 4.5 cm diam.; 8 x 8 cm total

● Photo p 10

Advice
Fold a variety of sizes and colors of the flowers and leaves. Affix to cards or postcards for a nice touch.

Flower

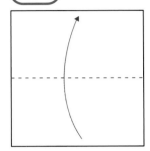

1
Fold in half.

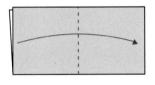

2
Fold in half again.

3
Crease all of it along the diagonal.

4
Cut off small section of all layers along solid line. Unfold entirely.

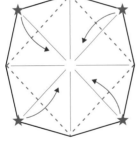

5
Fold ★ corners towards center aligned with creases that radiate from the center.

Flip

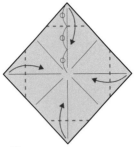
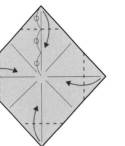

6
Flip over. Valley fold all four corners toward the center, about a third of the way in.

Flip

Done

Leaves

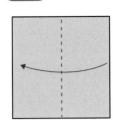

1
With front up, valley fold in half.

Enlarged

2
Cut along solid line according to diagram. Unfold. (You can trace the pattern with a pencil.)

Done

Iris ● Photo p 10, 69

Difficulty >> 😊 😊 😊

Paper size: Flower: 6 x 6 cm
　　　　　Leaves: 1 x 12 cm (2 sheets); 1 x 10 cm (2 sheets)
Finished size: Flower, 4.5 cm diam.; 17 cm tall

Advice

This is a traditional origami pattern, beloved since old times. This pattern has no stem; just place the flower in the middle of the lined-up leaves.

Flower

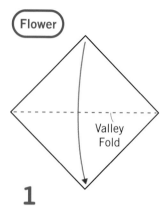

Valley Fold

1

Fold in half.

2

Valley fold side corners so that the ★ align with ☆.

Enlarged

Mountain Fold

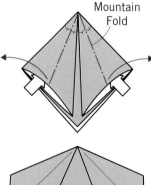

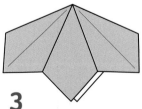

3

Open from bottom. Fold down along mountain fold lines.

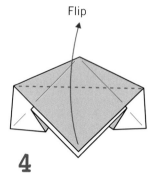

Flip

4

Flip over. Fold up top layer only as indicated.

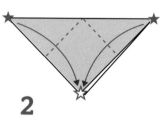

5

Valley fold along dashed line.

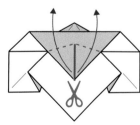

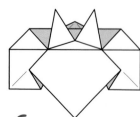

6

Cut where indicated on center piece only. Fold up on angled lines. Flip it over and you're done.

Leaves

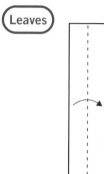

1

Fold in half along length.

✂

2

Cut off along solid line. Unfold. Make two large and two small leaves.

Done

Sunflower ● Photo p 11, 41

Difficulty >> 😊 😊 😊

Paper size: Flower: 15 x 15 cm
　　　　　Seeds: 7.5 x 7.5 cm　Leaves: 12 x 12 cm
Finished size: Flower, 10 cm diam.; 17 x 20 cm total

Advice

The reverse shows in the final flower, so use paper that's colored on both sides. The leaves are the same pattern as for the Curled Rose (p 51).
● Concept: Kyoko Nakahara

Flower

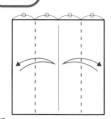

1
Crease in half along length. Fold edges to center line and unfold.

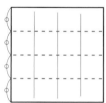

2
Repeat along width, creasing horizontally.

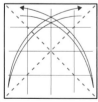

3
Next, crease along the diagonals.

Flip

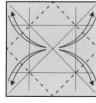

4
Flip over. Fold as if gathering corners to center then unfold.

Flip

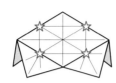

5
Flip over. Push in four ☆ to dent in.

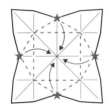

6
Fold up along creases so the ★ on the sides come to the center.

7
Holding down center, open and fold in the four corners so it ends up as pictured in step 8.

Enlarged

8
Crease all four corners with valley folds.

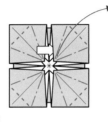

9
Open middle and fold flat all four corners.

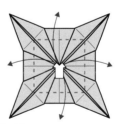

10
Pick up tips in center and fold outward along dashed lines.

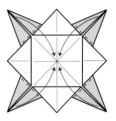

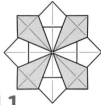

11
Fold all four triangular tips to center.

Seeds

Enlarged　Flip

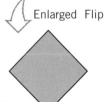

12
Fold corners to center. Flip over and the seeds are done.

13
Place the seeds at the center of the flower and insert at arrows.

Chrysanthemum ● Photo p 12

Difficulty >> 😊 😊 😊

Paper size: Flower: Large, 15 x 7.5 cm (12 sheets); Medium, 11.5 x 5.5 cm (12 sheets);
Small, 9 x 5 cm (18 sheets), 6 x 6 cm (1 sheet)
Base (craft paper): Large, 7 cm diam.; Medium, 6 cm diam.; Small, 5 cm diam. (1 each)
Leaves: Large, 15 x 7.5 cm (4 sheets); Small, 11.5 x 5.6 cm (4 sheets)   Stem: 10 x 10 cm (1 sheet)
Finished size: Flower, 17 cm diam.; 30 cm tall

(Flower)

Valley Fold

1

Place paper portrait-style.
Fold in half.

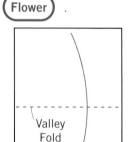

2

Fold in half again.

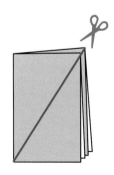

3

Cut along solid line.

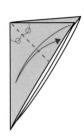

4

Crease top layer only
along dashed line.

Mountain Fold

5

Open top layer and
fold down. Repeat
with bottom.

↘ Enlarged

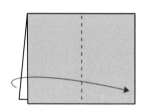

6

Crease according to
diagram. Repeat with
reverse side.

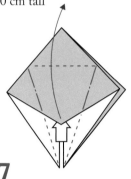

7

Open from bottom, fold
up corner, and fold flat.
Repeat with reverse side.

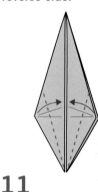

8

Fold down top layer only.
Repeat with reverse side.

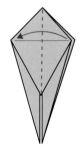

9

Fold right side of top
layer only to the left along
dashed line. Repeat with
reverse side.

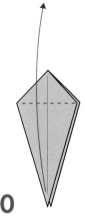

10

Fold top layer only
upwards. Repeat with
reverse side.

11

Fold sides to meet at
the center. Repeat with
reverse side.

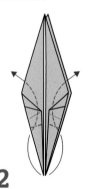

12

Inside reverse fold bottom
two tips (see p 19).

Advice

One flower is comprised of 51 wide-winged cranes. Curl one wing around a pencil to curve.
● Concept: Mitsuyo Matsumoto

● Combine ●

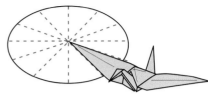

1

On each base paper, paste 12 cranes of equal size facing the same direction. On the small base, paste an additional 6 cranes inside others and the crane made from square paper in the center. Cut hole in large base only.

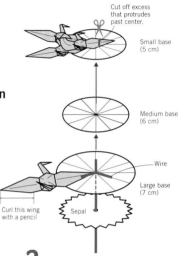

Cut off excess that protrudes past center.

Small base (5 cm)

Medium base (6 cm)

Wire

Large base (7 cm)

Curl this wing with a pencil

Sepal

2

Bundle three 35 cm lengths of wire. Insert through sepal and large base. Fold wires out into three directions and paste in place. Affix medium and small base papers, making sure cranes don't overlap. Curl outward wings.

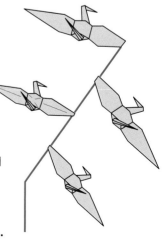

3

Wrap one wing of each leaf crane around wire, two large cranes followed by two small ones. Make two sets, bend wire as shown and attach 12 cm below sepal with floral tape.

(Sepal)

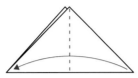

1

Fold into triangle. Fold in half along dashed line.

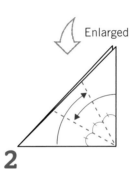

Enlarged

2

Fold the right angle into three equal angles.

3

Cut along solid line. Unfold. With the reverse face up, open a hole in the center so the stem can pass through.

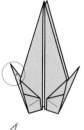

Enlarged

13

Inside reverse fold left tip again to create head.

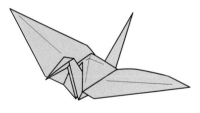

14

One crane done. Fold all flower and leaf papers into cranes. Follow the same instructions for the square paper, skipping step 3.

Cosmos ● Photo p 13

Difficulty >> 😊 😊 😊

Paper size: Flower, 3 x 18 cm; Leaves, 3 x 18 cm
Finished size: Flower, 5 cm diam.; 17 cm tall

● Photo p 13

Advice

Simply folding a slender piece of paper in half and cutting into it yields this many-petaled cosmos. Thin paper is best.

Flower

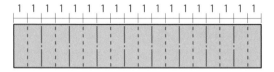

1

Alternate valley and mountain folds at 1 cm intervals to create 18 equal sections.

2

Fold ☆ to ★ at the base of the mountain folds, creasing along dashed lines.

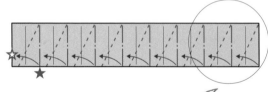

Enlarged

3

Following creases, fold in starting from edge so ★ aligns with ☆.

4

As you fold in the whole strip, it will curl up as shown. Overlap part A with part B to connect.

5

Cut along solid lines at each ○. Fold back triangular sections.

Leaves

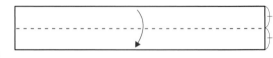

1

Fold in half along dashed line.

2

Make diagonal incisions at fine intervals, leaving just a bit at the looped arrow uncut.

3

Grasp both ends and twist well.

4

Cut flower petals according to diagram and glue to end of leaves.

Camellia ● Photo p 14, 57

Difficulty >> 😊 😊 😊

Paper size: Flower: 12 x 12 cm
Pistil: 3 x 10 cm
Leaves: 15 x 15 cm
Finished size: Flower, 6.5 cm diam.; 10 cm diam. total

Advice

The flower and leaves are made from one sheet of paper each. Make sure you fold firmly, even for small corners.

Flower

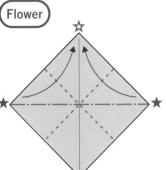

1

With front facing up, square fold (see p 19; fold from reverse).

Enlarged

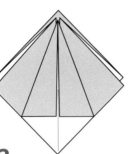
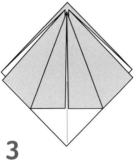

2

Crease along dashed lines to center.

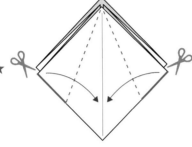

3

Cut along solid line. Fold along crease made in step 2. Repeat for the three other spots.

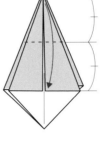

4

Fold down top layer only along dashed line. Repeat for the three other spots.

Enlarged

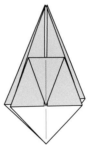

5

Fold both sides to align with ☆ and ★ lines. Repeat with reverse side.

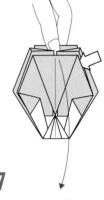

6

Fold all layers of bottom section up along dashed line.

7

Open and pull out the front to bloom.

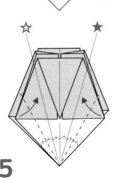

8

Mountain fold all eight tips.

Pistil

See the Plum Blossom pattern on p 75.

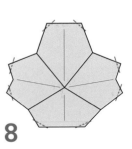

Continued on p 31

Poinsettia ● Photo p 15

Difficulty >> ☺ ☺ ☺

Paper size: Flower: 10 x 10 cm (2 sheets)
Leaves: 15 x 15 cm (2 sheets)
Finished size: 21 x 14 cm

Advice

Use sturdy paper for a splendid
Christmas decoration.
● Concept: Susumu Nakajima

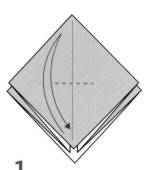

1

Square fold (see p 19).
Crease top layer only to
mark center.

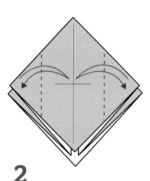

2

Valley fold left and right
corners to crease.

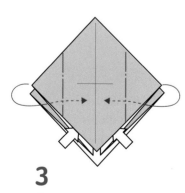

3

Open at arrow and fold in
along the crease.

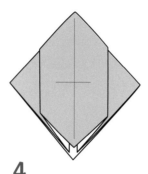

4

Repeat steps 1 to 3 on
reverse side.

5

Once you get the above
shape, unfold entirely.

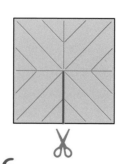

6

Cut along solid line.

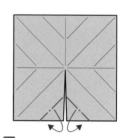

7

Fold back along
mountain fold lines.

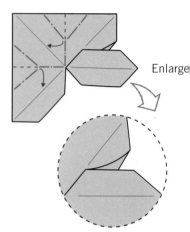

8

Carefully confirming
the lines above, fold so
mountain fold A aligns
with crease B.

Enlarge

9

Repeat with the other two
sections. The overlapping
parts should pop up
slightly.

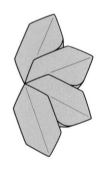

10

Once you get the above
shape, flip over.

Flip

Continued from p 29 ⟹

Camellia

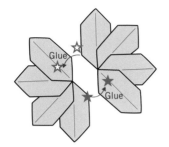

13

Flip over and glue together halves. Using creases as guides, glue together at ★ and ☆.

11

Open at arrows and fold down.

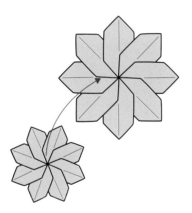

14

Glue flower to leaves. Paste pistil to center of flower and you're done.

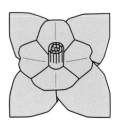

12

This is how it should look. Repeat with remaining flower paper and two leaf pieces.

Flip

(Leaves)

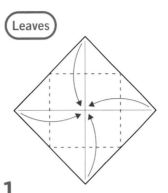

1

Valley fold along diagonals to crease, and fold corners to meet at the center.

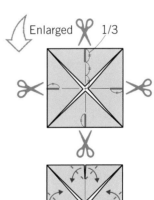

2

Cut four lines according to diagram one-third in from edge. Fold cut corners along dashed lines.

Leave margin

3

Fold in half along width, then fold back top layer only, leaving a margin. Repeat along the length.

Enlarged

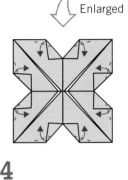

4

Valley fold along dashes to create subtle curves.

Flip

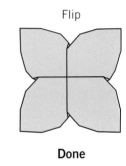

Done

● Combine ●

Paste pistil to center of flower. Position flower so the petals rest between the leaves and glue in place.

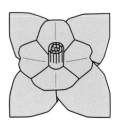

Done

Daffodil ● Photo p 16

Difficulty >> ☺ ☺

Paper size: Flower, 5 x 12 cm; Leaves, 3 x 28 cm (4 sheets)
Finished size: Flower, 7 cm diam.; 31 cm tall

The final twist on the bottom creates the flower petals and the pistil. Be sure to open up the pistil side well.
● Concept: Akemi Tatsumi

Flower

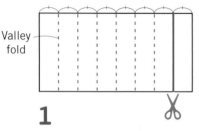

Valley fold

1

Valley fold to crease into eight equal parts. Cut off far right section.

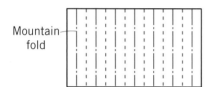

Mountain fold

2

Mountain fold along the middle of each creased section from step 1 to create an accordion shape.

Enlarged

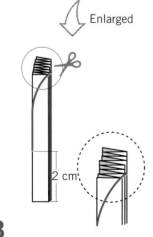

2 cm

3

Starting at the peaks of the mountain folds, cut along solid line according to the diagram. Be sure to start from the correct side.

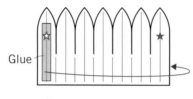

Glue

4

Open. Glue ☆ section and affix to front side of ★ section so the end petals overlap.

5

Fold along crease lines.

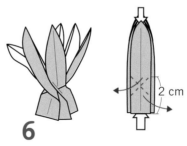

2 cm

6

Crease whole along dashed lines. Open top and bottom and twist firmly along creases.

Done

Leaves

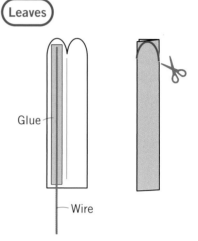

Glue

Wire

Fold in half along length, cut along solid line, and unfold. Affix wire to center, then glue and fold together halves.

● Combine ●

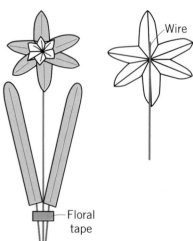

Wire

Floral tape

Affix wire to back of flower, combine with leaves, and wrap floral tape around base of wires.

For Expressing Your Feelings

Flower Gifts

Seeing them smile when they get a gift of flowers
makes the giver feel happy too, doesn't it?
Fold feelings of celebration, welcoming or gratitude
into these origami and turn them into lovely presents.

Roses

Anyone would be delighted to receive brilliant roses, for which there are a wide variety of origami patterns, each with unique instructions and final shapes.

Deluxe Rose

When it comes to gorgeous bouquets, many people immediately imagine a bunch of bright red roses. Tell them these stately ones are hand-crafted origami and see how impressed they'll be.

● Instructions p 49

Box Rose

These have a uniquely inorganic feel to them like the popular preserved flowers. The straight lines exude geometric beauty. Combine five boxes to create one flower.

● Instructions p 50

Curled Rose

These look like live rose buds. Simply curl up soft, thin paper to make these lovely flowers. Add lifelike leaves, stems and sepals to create a handsome bouquet.

● Instructions p 51

Carnations

The flower of choice for Mother's Day helps you express
the gratitude that you're often unable to put into words.
Just one glance will make the recipient beam with joy,
and carnations linger in the world of memory.

Double Carnation

These three-dimensional
carnations can be turned into
a bouquet with the addition of
stems and leaves. Simply fold
using two sheets of paper to
give volume to the frilly petals.

● Instructions p 52

Carnation

These are small and sweet. Paste to card stock and create your own Mother's Day card. This pattern is so easy even kids can make it.

● **Instructions p 53**

Lily

Lilies are defined by their distinctive trumpet shape and elegantly curled tips. Just one sheet of paper will yield a pretty lily with perfect petals.

 Instructions p 54

Bellflower

These small flowers bloom facing down, as if in modesty. The secret to creating their pretty silhouette is to not open the petals too much. Pass a wire through several flowers to make a corsage.

● Instructions p 55

Wrappings

Even a single origami flower can make simple gift wrapping markedly more elegant. Use these to dress up pastry as well as precious gifts.

Stacked Rose

This flat rose is very
convenient for use on boxes.
The stacked petals are simply
a smaller set nested within a
larger set of the same design,
so it's very easy to make.

● **Instructions p 56**

Curled Rose

Aside from decorations,
curled roses can be used as
soft packing material for
presents. Use to keep items
balanced or to protect fragile
things inside a gift box.

● **Instructions p 51**

Brooches

If you fold them well using sturdy paper, origami flowers that include details like pistils and leaves turn into excellent brooches. They make for modest gifts that will surely delight both children and adults.

Lily Brooch

Make a lily on the large side and add a pistil to make it even more realistic and gorgeous. A stem and leaves complete a sophisticated design perfectly suited to formal clothes.

● Instructions p 57

Camellia Brooch

With its vivid yet classy colors, a camellia brooch can lend an understated outfit a touch of verve. Use paper that has some resilience.

● Instructions p 57

Sunflower Brooch

When meticulously crafted to smaller specifications than the ebullient oversized version, the sunflower design yields a cute brooch. Stick this on a summery jute tote.

● Instructions p 57

Flower Cards

If it's too daunting or you're too shy to draw a picture on a card, then we highly recommend adding origami flowers instead. If you mail it, be sure to place it in an envelope and not as a postcard.

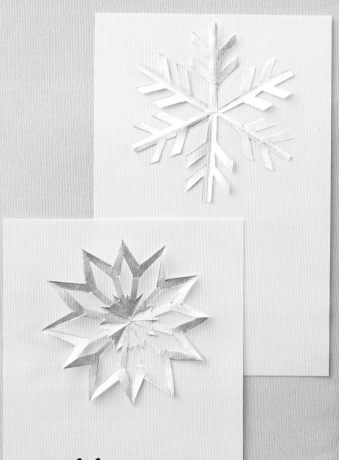

Maple
Simply fold and cut to create these sharp, pretty leaves. Enjoy the thrill that comes from unfolding these.

● Instructions p 58

Snowflake
Make a simple yet stylish Christmas card. Use the same fold but different cuts to create a variety of shapes.

● Instructions p 58

暑中お見舞い申し上げます

謹賀新年

Small Morning Glory

Make these wide-open morning glories in a variety of sizes and colors and affix them to a card along with the leaves for a painterly image. Use papers with gradient for a truly stylish look.

● Instructions p 59

Plum Blossom

While these elaborate pink and white plum blossoms feature five petals plus pistils, they're not difficult to make. Add them to a greeting card for a lasting impression.

● Instructions p 59

Wall Hangings

Origami flowers are fun just to make, but why not try using fine papers to fold a complete flower to display on the wall? It's easy to change it out to match the season, too.

Tulip

Hang these adorable tulips on the wall to brighten the entire room. The simple design allows the texture of the stock to come to the fore; the version pictured uses paper with a gradient wash.

● Instructions p 60

Hydrangea

With their full, round, brightly colored blossoms, hydrangeas are somehow nostalgic. Combine small flowers of three colors and use a green paper napkin to create soft leaves.

● Instructions p 61

Gift Envelope (Rose)

A handmade gift envelope adorned with an elegant flower imparts a warmer sense of celebration. Use a strip of red paper as an accent and to bind shut.

● **Instructions p 62**

Gift Envelope (Cherry Blossom)

This gift envelope uses high-quality paper and a fold that's been around since olden times. Add double-flowered cherry blossoms for a delicately florid finish.

● **Instructions p 63**

Flower Paper Case

These are perfect for gift money or for storing medicine. Traditional Japanese paper cases are called *tatou*, shortened from *tatamigami* ("folding paper"). You can open and refold them so they can be reused multiple times.

● Instructions p 64

Wrapping Bouquets

When you give origami flowers, be sure to wrap them like a real bouquet.
Wrapping is typically used to protect delicate blossoms, but in the case of
origami flowers, the paper frames and enhances the folded flowers.

Half Wrap

Wrap so the top is only half covered, allowing
the flowers to be seen even when the bouquet
is laid flat. Measure out wrapping paper to
half the circumference of the full bouquet and
wrap around the stems. White paper makes
the colors of the blooms pop.

Round Doily

This is a way to dress up the flowers
much like wrapping. Take a round doily
and cut from one point to the center.
At approximately the midpoints of
the bundled stems, overlap doily ends
slightly and fasten.

A Pretty Wrapping for Live Bouquets

**A florist will
protect your
bouquet with
clear film. It's
surprisingly
difficult to
wrap your own
bouquets. Use
these tips so
that the flowers
are protected
and still look
lovely.**

1
Where to place it
on the paper is key.
Lay at an angle
slightly in from
the corner with the
stems protruding.
Try folding up the
bottom corner to
see if it can be
folded back neatly
and adjust as need
be.

2
Never move the
bouquet. The
paper is the right
size if you can fold
back the opposite
side generously as
shown. Keeping
the top layer folded
back, wrap around
stems and tape in
place.

Deluxe Rose ● Photo p 34

Difficulty >> 😊 😊 😊

Paper size: Petals: Large, 17 x 6 cm (4 sheets); Small, 15 x 5 cm (9 sheets)
Sepal: 12 x 12 cm   Leaves: 5 x 5 cm (3 sheets)
Finished size: Flower, 11 cm diam. ; 35 cm total

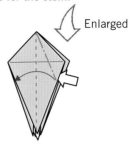

Advice

Use flexible paper that's colored on both sides. Bundle three pieces of 20-gauge wire and wrap with floral tape for the stem.

Flower

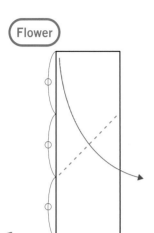

1

Gently bend top section at a right angle about a third up from the bottom.

2

Gently bend in half along width as shown.

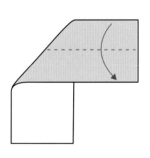

3

Gently bend down along dashed line without creasing so ★ aligns with ☆. Staple in place as shown on right.

4

Repeat with remaining flower petals. Wrap two small petals around curled ends of stem wires and bind with 30-gauge wire.

5

Applying glue to the bottom end of each petal, attach. Add large petals.

Leaves

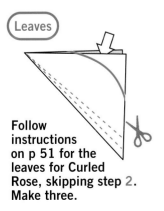

Follow instructions on p 51 for the leaves for Curled Rose, skipping step 2. Make three.

Sepal

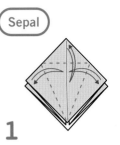

1

Square fold (see p 19). Rotate as shown and crease along dashed lines.

2

Open top layer. Fold up and flatten.

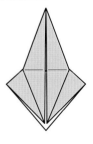

3

This is how it should look. Repeat with reverse side.

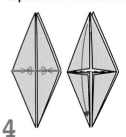

4

Cut along solid lines on top layer only. Fold down top corner. Repeat with reverse side.

Enlarged

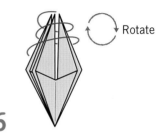

5

Open at arrow and fold flat. Repeat with remaining three sides.

Rotate

6

Rotate 180°. Twist top half a few times to curl.

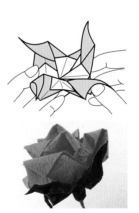

7

Open from center. Cut a hole in the bottom, insert wire and glue in place. Bind until dried, then remove binding.

● Combine ●

Follow instructions on p 51 for Curled Rose and combine three leaves with the stem.

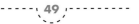

Box Rose ● Photo p 35

Difficulty >> 😊 😊 😊

Paper size: Petals: 15 x 15 cm, 11 x 11 cm, 8 x 8 cm,
5.5 x 5.5 cm, 4 x 4 cm
Finished size: Flower, 7.5 cm diam.

● Photo p 35

Advice

Use sturdy craft paper. Make boxes of different sizes then combine five to create one flower.

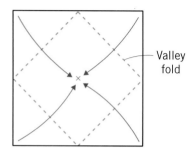

Valley fold

1

Mark center point. Fold all corners to the center.

Enlarged ↑ ↻ Rotate

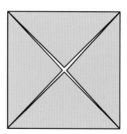

This is how it should look.

Flip

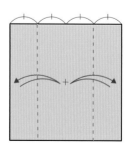

2

Fold left and right edges to the center to crease, then unfold.

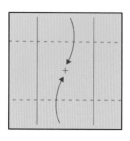

3

Fold top and bottom edges to the center.

Enlarged

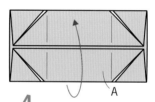

A

4

Bring up section A only.

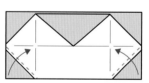

5

Fold up bottom corners.

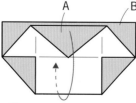

A   B

6

Fold A back down and under. Repeat steps 4-6 with section B.

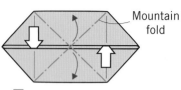

Mountain fold

7

Mountain fold to crease, and open and fold flat upward and downward as shown.

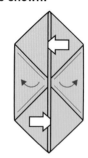

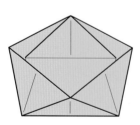

8

Firmly holding down crease, open into three-dimensional box. Repeat with remaining papers until you have five boxes.

● **Combine** ●

Nest progressively smaller boxes inside larger ones, alternating orientation with each box.

Curled Rose ● Photo p 35, 39

Difficulty >> 😊 😊 😊

Paper size: Flower: 25 x 25 cm   Sepal: 7.5 x 7.5 cm
Leaves: 4 x 4 cm (2 sheets), 5 x 5 cm (1 sheet)
Finished size: Flower, 3.5 cm diam.; 30 cm tall

Advice ◄

Use either fine *washi* paper or
even paper napkins. If using
two-ply napkins, separate layers
before folding.

Flower

1
Separate layers if using
two-ply napkins.

4
Remove chopstick. Glue
down end of paper without
crushing flower shape.

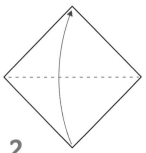

2
Fold into triangle.

3
Add a tiny dab of glue
to the tip of a chopstick.
Place tip at ★ and slowly
twirl paper.

Sepal

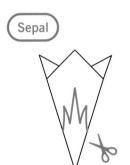

1
Follow steps **1-6** on p 20
for Cherry Blossoms. Cut
along solid line.

2
Unfold. Cut along solid
line to the center.

Leaves

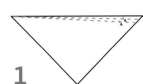

1
Fold into triangle and roll
fold edge.

2 Open
Pleat fold, mountain and valley
folding in turn, then open up.

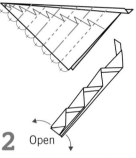

3
Cut off top and bottom
corners. Glue roll-folded
section and insert wire.

Stem

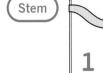

1
Glue top of a
piece of 20-gauge
wire and wrap
with a thin strip of
tissue paper.

2
Wrap with
floral tape.

Done

● Combine ●

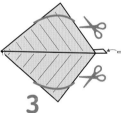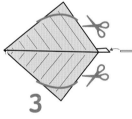

1
Insert stem through
center of flower and
glue in place. Wrap
sepal around base of
flower and fasten.

Glue

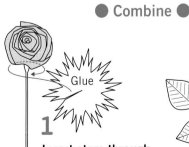

2
Combine 3
leaves and
attach to
stem using
floral tape.

Double Carnation ● Photo p 36

Difficulty >> 😊 😊 😊

Paper size: Flowers: 15 x 15 cm (2 sheets)   Sepal: 4 x 4 cm
Leaves: 5 x 1.2 cm (2 sheets)
Finished size: Flower, 7 cm diam.; 35 cm tall

Advice

These three-dimensional carnations are made by folding two sheets of paper together. Change up the colors to create a variety of looks.

Flower

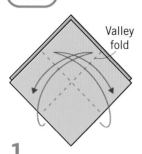

Valley fold

1

Stack two sheets front facing up. Fold both along center to crease.

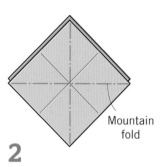

Mountain fold

2

Mountain fold along diagonals to crease.

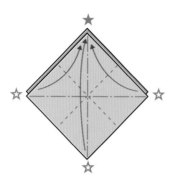

★ ☆   ☆ ★
☆

3

Gather and fold up the two side ☆ and bottom ☆ to align with ★.

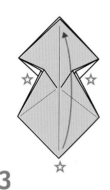

Enlarged

4

Fold side corners to center line. Repeat with reverse side.

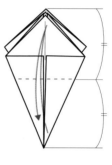

5

Crease at around the center of the whole shape.

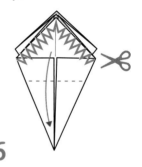

6

Cut along zig-zag line. Insert finger into top and pull open towards you.

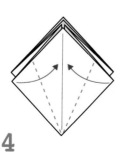

7

Open petals and fold, spreading out doubled petals.

Sepal

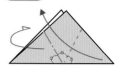

1

Fold into triangle. Valley and mountain fold where indicated into thirds.

2

Paste shut. Open at arrow and place flower inside.

Leaves

1

With the front facing up, fold in half along dashed line.

2

Cut along solid line. Cut in half to yield two leaves.

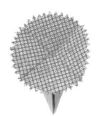

Carnation ● Photo p 37

Difficulty >> 😊 😊 😊

Paper size: Flower, 13 x 13 cm
Finished size: Flower, 6.8 cm diam.

● Combine ●

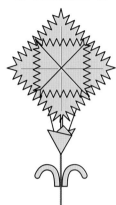

Cut hole in base of sepal. Curl tip of 20-gauge wire and insert. Paste flower, wire and sepal. Glue leaves to wire.

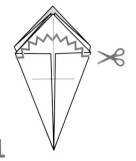

1

Follow steps 1-5 for Double Carnation on the previous page. Cut along zig-zag line.

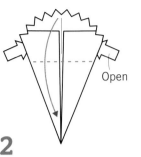

Open

2

Open, bringing top layer down towards you. Fold well.

Advice

This is the easiest of the flowers as well as the most versatile.
Use *washi* paper with a fine pattern or even wrapping paper for an adorable look.

Three Varieties of Flowers with One Design

There are countless thousands of origami designs,
but many share the same folding patterns until midway.
Have fun with a range of variations.

Made the same way as the Carnation, just with two sheets of paper. The finer the zig-zags, the more grown-up the impression.

Small Morning Glory

Instructions p 59

The simple Carnation shown on this page. You can use pinking shears for the zig-zag cut.

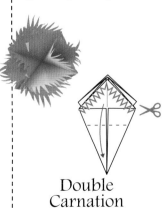

Double Carnation

Instructions p 52

Made with small paper. Broad curves yield the shape of a morning glory.

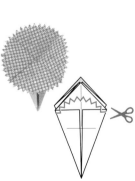

Carnation

Instructions p 53

Wrappings

Paste an origami flower on the knot in a ribbon,
or open a hole in the flower and pass a ribbon through.

Lily ● Photo p 38, 40

Difficulty >>

Paper size: 9 x 9 cm
Finished size: 7 cm diam.

Advice

This can be made using any type of paper, but the reverse side can show slightly in the center so use stock colored on both sides for best results.

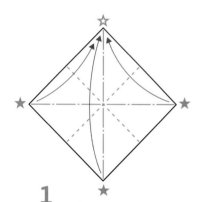

1

Align all ★ with ☆ to square fold (see p 19).

Enlarged

2

Crease, open and fold flat as shown. Repeat with three remaining sides.

3

Fold left and right corners to center to crease.

4

Open at arrow and fold down. Repeat with three remaining sides.

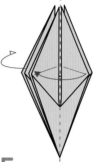

5

Fold top right layer to the left along the length. Repeat with three remaining sides.

6

Fold left and right corners to the center. It should look like the above. Repeat with three remaining sides.

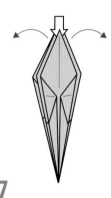

7

Open from the top and spread out petals.

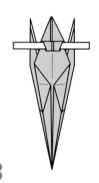

8

Wrap petal tips around a pencil to curl.

Done

Bellflower ● Photo p 38

Difficulty >> 😊 😊 😊

Paper size: 7 x 7 cm
Finished size: Flower, 3 cm diam.; 4 x 12 cm total

Advice

When you curl the petals, the reverse of the paper will show, so use stock colored on both sides for best results.

Flower

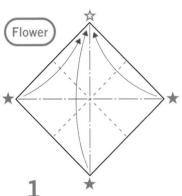

1

Align all ★ with ☆ to square fold (see p 19).

Enlarged

2

Open at arrow and fold down as shown. Repeat with three remaining sides.

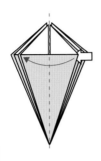

3

Fold top right layer to the left. Repeat with reverse side.

4

Fold top right and left corners only to center.

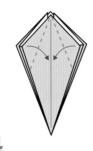

5

Fold to the left. Repeat step 4 with newly opened top layer. Repeat with two remaining sides.

6

Fold top right layer to the left. Repeat with reverse side.

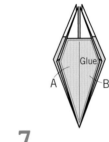

Glue
A   B

7

Glue parts A and B together. Return shape to step 6. Repeat with three remaining sides.

8

Wrap petal tips around a pencil to curl.

9

Open from the top, arranging to create a vase-like shape.

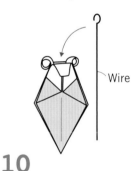

Wire

10

Curl one end of a piece of 22-gauge wire. Insert other end through flower.

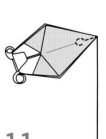

11

Bend flower at the bottom and you're done.

Stacked Rose ● Photo p 39

Difficulty >>

Paper size: Large, 15 x 15 cm; Small, 7.5 x 7.5 cm
Finished size: 7.5 x 7.5 cm

● Photo p 39

The small flower fits perfectly inside the large one. Use paper colored on both sides.

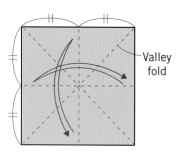

Valley fold

1

With front facing up, crease along dashed lines.

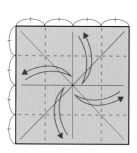

2

Crease along dashed lines, quartering each quadrant.

Flip

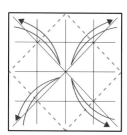

3

Flip over. Fold each corner to the center to crease.

Flip

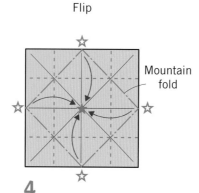

Mountain fold

4

Flip over. Using the creases, fold in all ☆ to align with ★. Fold new corners to the center.

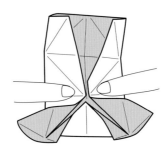

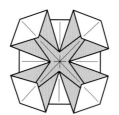

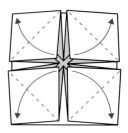

5

Fold top layers only along dashed lines.

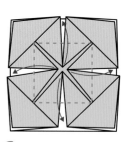

6

Fold inner triangular sections outwards and the flower part is done.

● Combine ●

Make one small and one large set of petals. Paste small petals inside large ones.

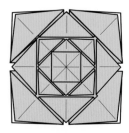

Done!

Lily Brooch ● Photo p 40

Difficulty >>

Paper size: Flower, 12 x 12 cm; Pistil, 6 x 6 cm;
Leaves, 5 x 1.5 cm (2 sheets)
Finished size: Flower, 7 cm diam.; 6.5 x 10 cm total

Flower

Follow instructions for Lily on p 54.

Leaves

1
Fold in half along length.

2
Cut along solid line. Unfold.

Leaf done.

Pistil

1
Follow steps 1-3 for Lily (p 54).

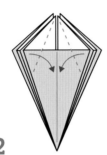

2
Fold side corners to the center.

3
This is how it should look. Repeat with three remaining sides and the pistil is done (as shown right).

● Combine ●

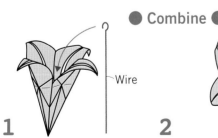

Wire

1
Cut a 10-cm length of wire, curl one end and insert into lily. Paste pistil inside flower. Bend wire at base of flower.

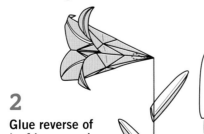

Glue

2
Glue reverse of leaf bases and wrap around wire. Affix brooch pin (see inset at right).

Instructions for Brooches

Lily Brooch

Camellia Brooch

Sunflower Brooch

Make 10-cm versions of the flowers plus leaves (see p 25 for Sunflower and p 29 for Camellia). Simply add brooch pin to the back. Coat front with clear nail polish to reinforce.

● Materials

Prep an origami flower, a brooch pin, and a 2 x 2 cm piece of heavy paper. Tools: Scissors and double-sided tape.

1
Affix double-sided tape to both faces of heavy paper and cut to fit the brooch pin. Attach heavy paper followed by pin to the back of the flower.

2
Use leftover heavy paper to cover back of pin in a cross shape.

Snowflake ● Photo p 42

Difficulty >> 😊 😊 😊

Paper size: 7.5 x 7.5 cm
Finished size: 7 cm diam.

● Photo p 42

Advice
Fold in half to crease to get accurate measurements without having to use a ruler.
● Concept: Hiromi Watabe

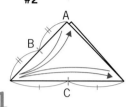

1

With front facing up, fold into a triangle. Mark at points B and C halfway on each side.

2

Mark point D, halfway between A and B.

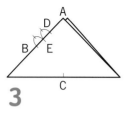

3

Mark point E, halfway between D and B.

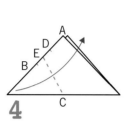

4

Valley fold along line joining E and C.

5

Valley fold along folded edge.

Enlarged

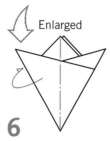

6

Mountain fold whole piece in half.

7

Cut as indicated by patterns to the right and unfold.

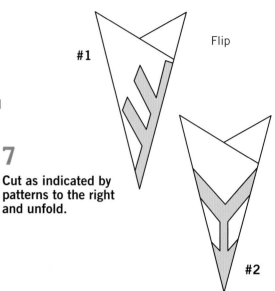

#1

Flip

#2

- -

Maple ● Photo p 42

Difficulty >> 😊 😊 😊

Paper size: 9 x 9 cm
Finished size: 7 x 11 cm

● Photo p 42

Advice
Keep the final cuts neat to make a beautiful, lifelike maple leaf.

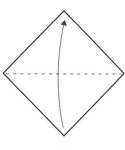

1

Fold into a triangle, then in half again.

2

Valley fold bottom corner to top. Repeat with reverse side. Unfold back to step 1.

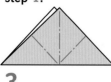

3

Mountain fold along valley-fold creases to alter crease.

4

4. Step fold (see p 18) so ★ lines are staggered.

Flip ↺ Rotate

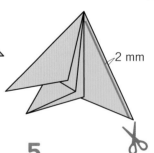

5

Flip over and cut along line. Flip back up.

Flip ↺ Rotate

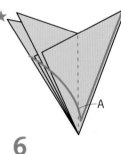

2 mm

A

6

Reinsert scissors at base of cut. Cut parallel to side ★ up to point A, then cut on a curve as shown. At the end, once the scissor tips run past the paper, cut off in a straight line. Unfold.

Small Morning Glory ● Photo p 43

Difficulty >>

Paper size: Flower: 4.5 x 4.5 cm
Leaves: 2 x 2 cm
Finished size: Flower, 2 cm diam.

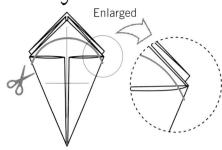

Enlarged

Using just one sheet of paper, follow steps 1-5 on p 52 (Double Carnation). Cut along solid line and unfold. Leaves: Follow instructions on p 23 (Morning Glory).

Plum Blossom ● Photo p 43

Difficulty >>

Paper size: 6 x 6 cm (2 sheets)
Finished size: 4 cm diam.

Advice

Fold one sheet into four petals, then add a fifth to create a plum blossom. Use paper colored on both sides for best results.
● Concept: Susumu Nakajima

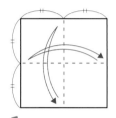

1
Crease along dashed lines.

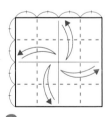

2
Crease along dashed lines.

Flip

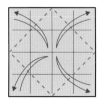

3
Fold corners to center to crease.

Flip

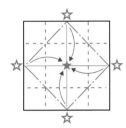

4
Flip over. Fold in all ☆ along creases to align with ★.

5
Fold new corners to the center.

Enlarged

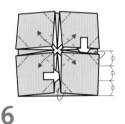

6
Lift open each quadrant slightly and mountain and valley fold as indicated.

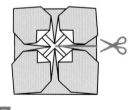

7
Cut along solid line to the center.

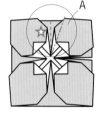
Enlarged

A

8
Under part A, mountain fold then valley fold in between. Slightly overlay part A on ☆. Repeat with two remaining sections.

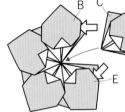

9
Repeat steps 1-6 with other sheet of paper and cut off one petal. Insert so parts C and D are under parts B and E, respectively, and paste.

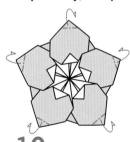

10
Fold back tips of petals.

Done

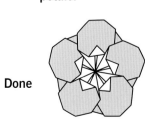

Wall Hangings

After folding origami, arrange on a base of card stock or construction paper and affix so the composition looks balanced.

Tulip ● Photo p 44

Difficulty >>

Paper sizes: Flower: 7.5 x 7.5 cm
Leaves: 10 x 10 cm
Finished size: 11 cm tall

Advice

The instructions are very simple but nail the signature shape of a tulip. The reverse of the paper will show slightly at the petal tips.

Flower

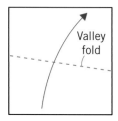

1
Fold at a slight slant.

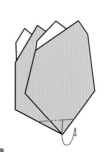

4
Fold back corner of the whole piece.

2
Fold once again at a slight slant.

5
Flower done.

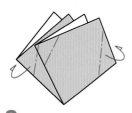

3
Fold back three corners along the indicated lines.

Leaves

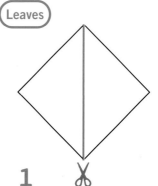

1
Fold in half along diagonal to crease, then cut.

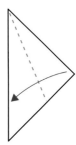

2
Fold in corner so it overlaps the vertical edge.

3
Fold in bottom as well.

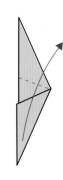

4
Fold up at a slight slant.

5
Fold back the bottom left corner.

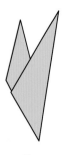

Done

Hydrangea ● Photo p 45

Difficulty >> 😊 😊 😊

Paper sizes: Flower: 4 x 4 cm (18 to 20 sheets)
Leaves: 11 x 11 cm (2 sheets)
Finished size: Flower, 3 cm diam.; 20 cm total

Advice

Combining different shades of a uniform color scheme adds depth to these handsome hydrangeas.

Flower

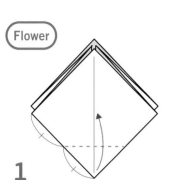

1

With reverse facing up, square fold (see p 19). Fold up according to diagram.

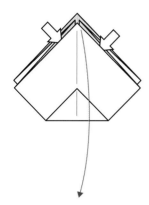

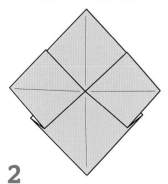

2

Open, and pull top layer towards you.

Flip

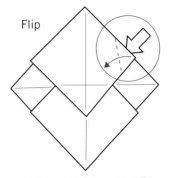

3

On reverse, valley fold as shown, then open and fold a triangle as in photo. Repeat with three remaining sections.

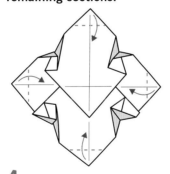

4

Valley fold all four corners.

Flip

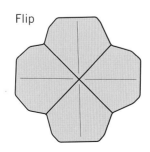

Done

Leaves

Follow steps 1-3 for leaves on p 51 (Curled Rose). Instead of adding wire, just paste overlapping sections in place.

● Combine ●

Fold 18 to 20 flowers and 2 leaves to create one hydrangea. Paste leaves to base paper, then glue on flowers in a circle, each slightly overlapping the next.

● Also: The Clover ●

Fold one hydrangea flower using green paper and add a thin long stem for a four-leaf clover. Use on cards or wall hangings, too.

Gift Envelope (Rose) ● Photo p 46

Difficulty >> ☺ ☺ ☺

Paper size: Envelope: 25 x 45 cm
Flower: 7 x 7 cm
Finished size: Flower, 4.2 cm diam.; Envelope, 10 x 17.5 cm

● Photo p 46

Advice

The color of the reverse of the paper for the envelope acts as an accent and a binding. Use stock colored on both sides for both the envelope and the rose.

Envelope

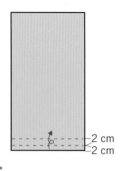

2 cm
2 cm

1

With front facing up, roll fold bottom edge (see p 18).

Flip

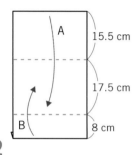

A

15.5 cm

17.5 cm

B

8 cm

2

Flip over. Fold down section A first, then fold up section B.

Enlarged

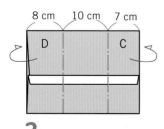

8 cm   10 cm   7 cm

D   C

3

Mountain fold C first, then D.

Flip

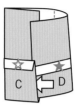

C   D

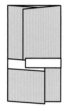

4

Open up section C and insert section D. Insert ☆ under ★.

Flip

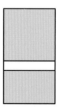

Done

Flower

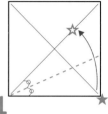

1

Crease along diagonals, then fold so ★ aligns with ☆.

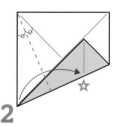

2

Repeat with bottom left corner, folding up to ☆.

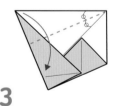

3

Repeat with top left corner.

Rotate

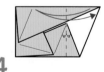

4

Crease final corner along dashed line.

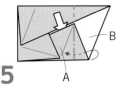

5

Slightly unfold section A and inside reverse fold (see p 19) section B .

Enlarged

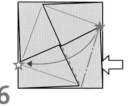

6

Open at arrow. Mountain fold so ★ aligns with ☆.

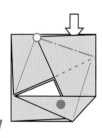

7

Repeat step 6, inserting ○ into ●. Repeat with two remaining sections.

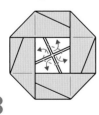

8

Valley fold back inner corners.

Done

Gift Envelope (Cherry Blossom)

Difficulty >> 😊 😊 😊

● Photo p 46

Paper size: Envelope: 34 x 40 cm
Flower: 4.5 x 4.5 cm (4 sheets), 4 x 4 cm (2 sheets)
Finished size: Envelope, 10 x 17.5 cm

Envelope

10 cm 10 cm 10 cm 4 cm

A

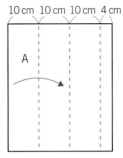

1

Crease along dashed lines. Fold section A only.

Enlarged

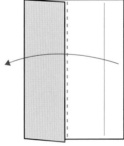

2

Valley fold to overlap.

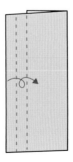

3

Roll fold protruding section (see p 18).

Advice

When using heavy paper, place a ruler on the inside of the fold to create a crisp crease. Be sure to get the final folding order right.

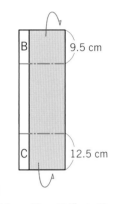

B   9.5 cm

C   12.5 cm

4

Fold section B first, then C.

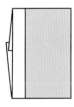

Done

Flower

Follow instructions on p 20 (Cherry Blossom) to make a triple cherry blossom. Stack and glue together. Affix two sets to envelope.

Flower Paper Case ● Photo p 47

Difficulty >> 😊 😊 😊

Paper size: 15 x 15 cm
Finished size: 8 cm diam.

● Photo p 47

Advice

As you fold it up, be sure to confirm the width of the section you're holding down.

1

Square fold (see p 19) and rotate.

(see p 19)

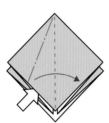

2

Fold corner along center line to crease, then open and fold flat. Repeat with three remaining sides.

3

Fold down top section of whole piece along width to crease. Unfold entirely.

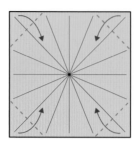

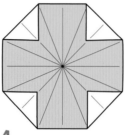

4

With front facing up, fold in all four corners.

Flip ↺ Rotate

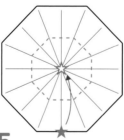

5

Flip over. Create eight creases as shown so that ★ will come to the center (☆), and start folding up.

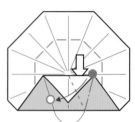

Hold down here only

6

Valley fold from the center, lifting at arrow, so that ● aligns with ○. The trick is to hold down just two sections.

7

Repeat seven times. At the end, open first fold and insert final fold underneath.

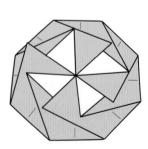

Done

For Everday Use and for Hosting

Practical Flowers

These pleasing origami are useful additions to the dinner table, etc.,
not to speak of just being lovely to look at.
The flower plates create a more relaxed atmosphere than fine china
and can be sent home with your guests.

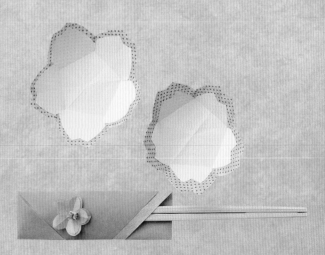

Using Paper Napkins

Paper napkins are thin and pliant, yet don't tear easily,
making them very useful for origami.
These are a way to add to the fun of snacktime.

Flower Napkin

Transform a colorful,
handy paper napkin into
a floral dish in just a few
folds! Use as a coaster or
to hold nuts or snacks.

● Instructions p 72

Lace Flower Case

A flower-shaped case for storing small items looks even lovelier when you fold it out of a doily. The lace pattern at the edges will show on the petals.

● Instructions p 73

Leaf Plate

For these tree leaf-shaped
origami dishes, try stacking
large pieces together to create
a luncheon placemat. These are
perfect for hikes or outdoor
picnics.

● **Instructions p 74**

Chopsticks Envelope
(Iris / Plum)

These chic chopsticks envelopes with
the diagonal lines are upgraded to a
classy table setting with the addition
of a small folded flower. Use them for
meals at seasonal celebrations.

● Instructions p 75

Cherry Blossom
Chopsticks Rest

The same origami cherry blossoms
can have a variety of uses. Simply
paste two offset blossoms together
for a posh chopsticks rest. Take these
with you on picnics.

● Instructions p 74

Flower Dish
(Cherry Blossom)

These cherry blossom-shaped dishes are very useful, large or small. Featuring overlaid cherry blossoms, they look especially casual and fresh if you use patterned paper.

● **Instructions p 76**

Flower Dish (Chrysanthemum)

Each individual petal is a separate dish. When pasted together at the center, they turn into a single flower that lends emphasis to the table.

● Instructions p 77

Flower Napkin ● Photo p 66

Difficulty >> 😊 😊 😊

Paper size: 16.5 x 16.5 cm
Finished size: 12 x 12 cm, 9 x 9 cm

Advice

The final turn-out might tear
the paper, so be sure to use
pliant stock or cloth napkins.

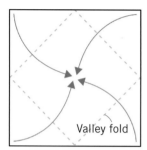

Valley fold

1

Mark the center. Fold
all four corners to the
center.

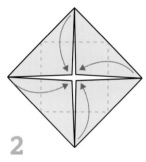

2

Fold new corners to the
center.

Enlarged

3

This is how it should
look. Flip over.

Flip

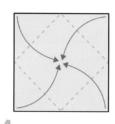

4

Again fold all four
corners to the center.

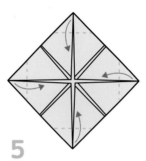

5

Fold in corners so it looks
like the picture below.

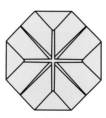

Flip

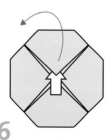

6

Flip over. Open at arrow
and fold out and back.

7

This is how it should
look. Hold down ★
with your thumb as
you fold out. With all
four corners done you
have the coaster.

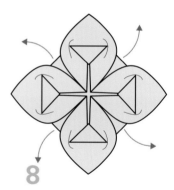

8

Fold the reverse layers
back upwards one at a
time as well and you'll
have a lush, round flower
shape.

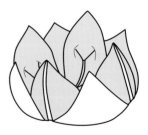

Done

Lace Flower Case ● Photo p 67

Difficulty >> 😊 😊 😊

Paper size: 20 x 20 cm
Finished size: 11 cm diam.

Advice

This requires some technique, so practice on plain paper first, then use a doily.
● Concept: Seiji Noma

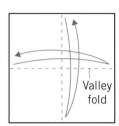

1
Crease along dashed lines.

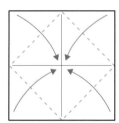

2
Fold corners to the center.

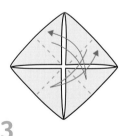

3
Crease whole piece along dashed lines.

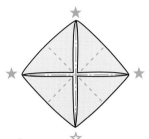

4
Make mountain-fold creases in a cross pattern. Fold so the ★ align with ☆.

Enlarged

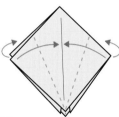

5
This is how it should look. Fold top layers to the center. Repeat with reverse side.

6
Open at arrow and fold as shown. Repeat with reverse side.

7
With all four places done as shown, crease well.

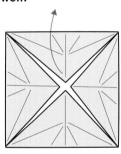

8
Unfold back to step 4, then unfold top section.

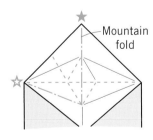

9
Using existing creases, fold the ★ mountain-fold line onto the ☆ line.

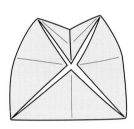

10
Use existing creases to fold point ★ down and in.

11
This is how it should look. Repeat steps 8-11 with three remaining sides.

Done

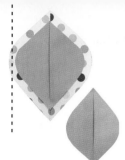

Leaf Plate

● Photo p 68

Difficulty >>

Paper size: Large, 20 x 20 cm; Small, 16 x 16 cm
Finished size: 27 x 21 cm

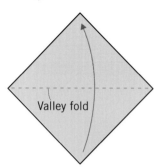

Valley fold

1

**With front facing up,
fold in half.**

3

**Cut both layers along
solid line to round the
leaf's edges.**

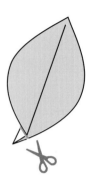

5

**Cut off protruding
section. Optionally,
glue center to keep
from unfolding.**

● **Change the Size** ●

**For a smaller dish,
use 10 x 10 cm of
heavyweight paper
for a finished size of
13.5 x 10 cm.**

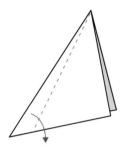

2

**Fold left edge
diagonally along
dashed line.**

Open
here

4

Open up.

Cherry Blossom Chopsticks Rest ● Photo p 69

Difficulty >>

Paper size: Large, 8 x 8 cm; Small, 6 x 6 cm

Finished size: 7.5 cm diam.

Follow instructions on p 20
(Cherry Blossom) and create
large and small versions.
Place small blossom askew
on larger blossom and paste
together in two places.

Chopsticks Envelope (Iris / Plum) ● Photo p 69

Difficulty >> 😊 😊 😊

Paper size: Envelope: 15 x 15 cm (both)
               Iris: 3.5 x 3.5 cm   Plum: Flower: 4 x 4 cm, 3.5 x 3.5 cm
                             Pistil: 6 x 0.8 cm
Finished size: Flowers, 3.5 cm diam.; Envelope, 4 x 13 cm

Advice

You actually make the envelope from a square piece of paper. Use stock that has a vivid reverse color so the slender line stands out.

Envelope

0.7 cm

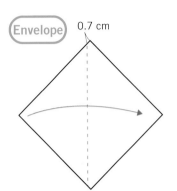

1
Fold into a triangle, slightly off-center.

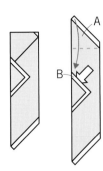

4
Valley fold section A, insert under section B, and paste in place.

Flower

See p 24 for instructions for Iris. Combine with leaves.

Follow steps 1-6 on p 20 (Cherry Blossom) to create two sizes of Plum Blossoms, cutting petals as shown. Stack blossoms and paste together at center, and glue pistil into center.

4 cm

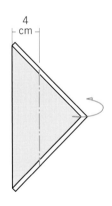

2
Mountain fold as shown.

Flip

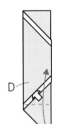

5
Valley fold section C and insert into section D.

Pistil

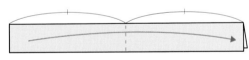

Done

1
Fold in half along horizontal axis, then along vertical axis.

2
Fold in half again.

Leave a margin

3
Cut along solid lines, leaving bottom uncut.

Glue

4 cm

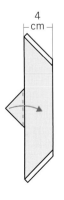

3
Valley fold protruding section.

4
Roll up. Glue to close coil and you're done.

Flower Dish (Cherry Blossom) ● Photo p 70

Difficulty >> 😊 😊 😊

Paper size: Large, 13 x 13 cm; Small, 12 x 12 cm
FInished size: 10 cm diam.

● Photo p 70

Advice

Use parchment paper for the small blossom and this dish will be oil-proof, allowing you to use it multiple times.

1

Create large and small versions of Cherry Blossoms (see p 20).

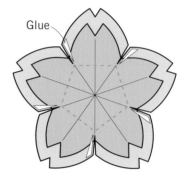

Glue

4

Valley fold, overlapping and pasting adjacent petals.

2

Glue reverse of small blossom and paste to center of large blossom.

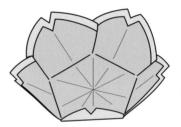

Done

3

Cut halfway into large blossoms as shown.

16 cm

10 cm

● Change the Size ●

The large version in the photo is made using 23 x 23 cm (large) and 21 x 21 cm (small) papers.

Flower Dish (Chrysanthemum) ● Photo p 71

Difficulty >> 😊 😊 😊

Paper size: 15 x 7.5 cm (6 sheets)
Finished size: 24 cm diam.

● Photo p 71

Advice ✒

Use paper colored on both sides. Be sure not to tear it when turning inside out.

 ↻ Rotate   Enlarged

1

Cut in half.

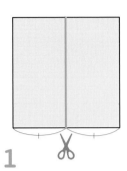

2

With front facing up, valley fold along dashed line, 1/7 of height from top edge.

1/7
Valley fold

3

Fold in half.

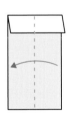

4

Fold both front and reverse in half outward.

5

Confirming the direction, valley fold top layer only of corners into triangles.

6

Valley fold again on the slant. Repeat with reverse side.

7

Open from top (top photo), and pushing in at ★, turn inside-out (bottom photo).

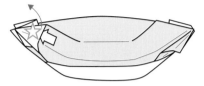

8

Lift up ☆ section.

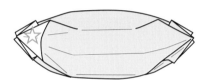

9

Petal done. Make six and glue together so the ☆ sections meet around the center.

Done

Tips for Pretty Presentation

Crisp folds give life to smooth, clean shapes and
allow for a wonderful finish. Get the hang of it!

Choose Easy-To-Use Sizes of Paper

Paper the size of your handspan is the easiest to work with.

For origami, paper that's as wide as your handspan is easiest to fold. For an adult, that's about 6~7 inches squared—the size of standard origami paper. The paper sizes very to enhance the charms of the designs, but try working with an easy size to start. Once you know the folds, you're less likely to botch it with a different size of paper.

Practice with large paper before attempting small designs

Hydrangea (p 61) made to our final specs requires 4 x 4 cm paper. The left is easy-to-use 15 x 15 cm paper.

This is how it looks partway folded. The smaller paper gets smaller as you go.

Where you open the fold, the small version on top is hard to see. All our instruction photos use 15 x 15 cm paper as in the bottom photo. For practice, use standard origami paper that's white on the reverse for ready comparison with our instructions.

Done. Practice with large paper then take on the challenge of making it with small paper.

Neatly Fit Corners and Edges Together

Check with fingertips

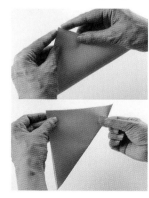

It's common to fold origami on a flat work surface, but in fact, it's easier to neatly align corners and edges with your fingertips if you hold it aloft at first. Touch with the pads of your fingers to make sure edges and corners meet properly. Hold corners together with one hand and crease with the other to prevent misalignment.

Create Crisp Creases

Use a handy wooden spatula

Creases are often used in later folds so it's important to make each one well. Take care to avoid refolding and creating double creases. Use a spatula to crease crisply with little effort.

Origami spatula

Think Twice When Cutting

Don't just glance at the diagram before cutting. It's important to confirm where the guideline creases are, etc. Read the directions and trace the line with a pencil. The slightest variance in the cut will create noticeable changes in the finished work.

Make Different Sizes

Different sizes of paper will result in origami with different impressions even when the design is the same. Try making different versions in a variety of sizes and combinations. However, when making origami such as Stacked Rose (p 56) or Box Rose (p 50) that use an assemblage of different sizes of paper, be sure to keep the ratios the same.

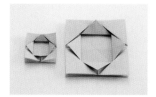

Choose Paper to Suit the Design

It's important to choose appropriate paper depending on whether the work will be used for decorating, gifting or serving food. Standard origami paper is white on the reverse, but for designs where the reverse is visible, use stock that's the same shade on both sides or *washi* with two different colors for a lovely finish. A good number of photos in this book feature origami folded with *washi* that evinces a very grown-up feel. Also try wrapping paper in pop patterns or soft, flexible paper napkins.

Washi

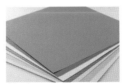

Regular paper

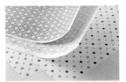

Wrapping paper

Paper napkins

Cut Paper Cleanly

When cutting paper down to the necessary size, it's important to create right angles and straight edges. When using large sheets such as wrapping paper, first cut down to easy-to-manage dimensions, then cut out the size needed for the design.

These are tools that make cutting easy. Rather than scissors, use a craft knife, ruler and cutting mat instead. A ruled cutting mat will make it easy to measure lengths and to cut perfect angles while protecting your table.

1
First cut wrapping paper or *washi* to an easily managed size.

2
Align ruler with lines on cutting mat and slice off for a clean edge.

3
Rotate paper 90° and slice off again. Proceed to cut down to necessary size.

For when you get stuck folding...

Double-check the symbols

Look carefully at the diagram and make sure you haven't missed arrows and other symbols or when to flip over. Check the legend (p 17-19) and verify what the symbols mean. Pay special attention to the front vs. reverse side and valley vs. mountain folds.

Crease along lines as indicated

Sometimes you'll make a valley-fold crease that you'll turn into a mountain-fold crease in a later step. Double-check as you fold and make sure you're creasing in the right place.

Always look one step ahead

Look at what the shape should be in the following step and fold with that shape in mind. Keep an eye on the coming picture and stay one step ahead.

◎ Profiles ◎

KAZUO KOBAYASHI

Board chairman: Officially-recognized NPO: International Origami Society.
Director: Ochanomizu Origami Kaikan. Born 1941.
Teaches origami classes at Ochanomizu Origami Kaikan and holds origami exhibits and lectures around
the world. Various appearances on TV and in the media have earned him a large number of fans.
Mr. Kobayashi has published several origami books.

*The washi paper shown in this book is provided by Kobayashi of Yushima LLC.
Some of the featured papers may no longer be available for purchase.

Kobayashi of Yushima (Ochanomizu Origami Kaikan)
Ochanomizu Origami Kaikan, 1-7-14 Yushima, Bunkyo-ku, Tokyo 113-0034
Tel: 03-3811-4025

YOSHIHIKO KOGA

Kyorin University: Professor of Neuropsychiatry.
Born 1946. Graduate of Keio University.
Board chairman: Officially-recognized NPO: Japan Brain Health Association.
Mr. Koga has supervised several publications.

Origami Flowers
Fold Beautiful Paper Bouquets

Product/Diagram Creation: Nobue Yuasa
Design: Mitsuhiro Wada
Photography: Tsutomu Hara
Styling: Noriko Yaguchi
Diagram Tracing: day studio
Editor: Aya Sakurai

Production: Hiroko Mizuno
Grace Lu

Hana no Origami
© 2008 Kazuo Kobayashi All rights reserved.

Translation © 2014 by Vertical, Inc.
Published by Vertical, Inc., New York

First published in Japan in 2008 by KADOKAWA SS Communications Inc.
English translation rights arranged with KADOKAWA

ISBN: 978-1-939130-18-1

Manufactured in Malaysia

First Edition

Vertical, Inc.
451 Park Avenue South, 7th Floor
New York, NY 10016
www.vertical-inc.com

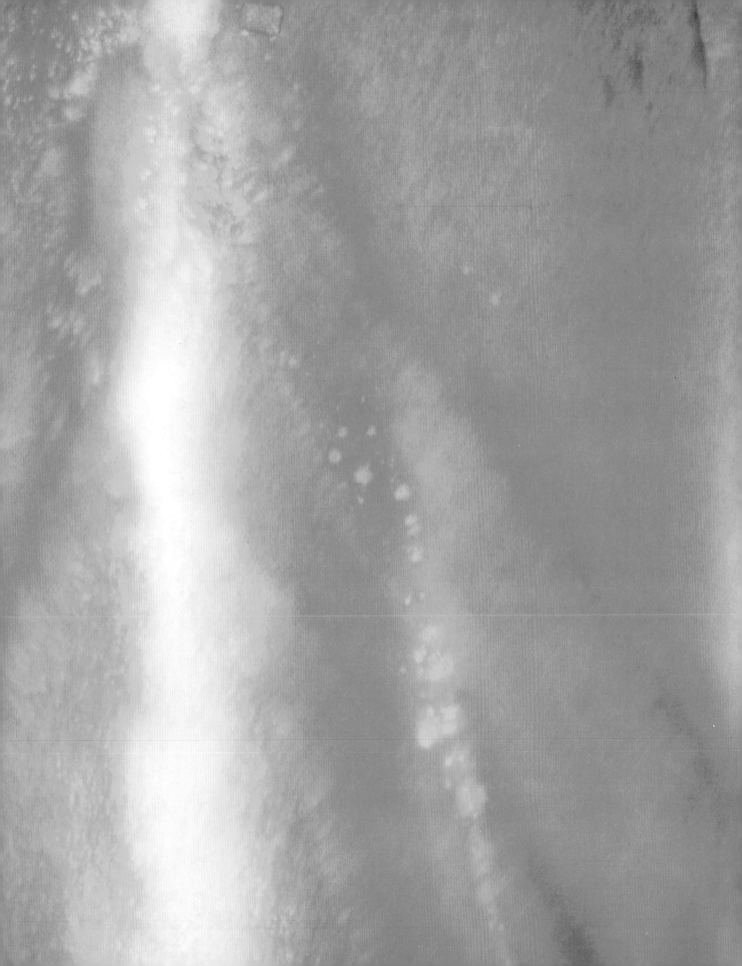